Contents

Things you can see in spring

buds

You can see **buds**.

Seasons

What Can You See in Spring?

Siân Smith

Raintree is an imprint of Capstone Global Library Limited, a company incorporated in England and Wales having its registered office at 7 Pilgrim Street, London, EC4V 6LB – Registered company number: 6695582

www.raintreepublishers.co.uk
myorders@raintreepublishers.co.uk

Edited by James Benefield and Kathryn Clay
Designed by Richard Parker
Picture research by Tracy Cummins
Production by Helen McCreath
Originated by Capstone Global Library Ltd
Printed and bound in China by Leo Paper Group

ISBN 978 1 406 28322 8 (hardback)
18 17 16 15 14
10 9 8 7 6 5 4 3 2 1

ISBN 978 1 406 28327 3 (paperback)
19 18 17 16 15
10 9 8 7 6 5 4 3 2 1

British Library Cataloguing in Publication Data
A full catalogue record for this book is available from the British Library.

Acknowledgements
We would like to thank the following for permission to reproduce photographs: Dreamstime.com: © Hupeng, 11, 22; iStockphoto: © aimintang, 7, © coramueller, 16, back cover, © Madzia71, 8, © Milan Zeremski, 15; Shutterstock: Algefoto, 17, Anne Kitzman, 9, ayosphoto, 20 middle, Drew Rawcliffe, 13, Franck Boston, 20 left, LittleStocker, 6, Matej Kastelic, 4, 22, Ozerov Alexander, 18, Pavel L Photo and Video, 20 right, Phant, 12, Richard Schramm, 21, Rtimages, 19, Simon Greig, 5, Smit, 14, Vlasta Kaspar, 10.

Cover photograph reproduced with permission of Shutterstock, © Peter Wey.

Every effort has been made to contact copyright holders of material reproduced in this book. Any omissions will be rectified in subsequent printings if notice is given to the publisher.

You can see daffodils.

You can see tulips.

blossoms

You can see blossoms.

bee

You can see bees.

nest

You can see nests.

You can see ducklings.

You can see **tadpoles**.

You can see piglets.

You can see lambs.

You can see rain.

You can see umbrellas.

You can see wellington boots.

puddle

You can see puddles.

You can see rainbows.

You can see kites.

Spring quiz

Which clothes would you wear in spring?

The four seasons follow a pattern.
Which season comes after spring?

spring

?

winter

autumn

Picture glossary

 **bud**

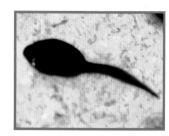 **tadpole**

Index

Answer to quiz on page 20: rain coat
Answer to question on page 21: summer

Notes for teachers and parents

Before reading

Building background: Talk about the seasons of the year. Which season are we in at the moment? Ask children what they would see if they looked out of a window in spring.

After reading

Recall and reflect: Which season is before spring? Which season follows spring? What is the weather like in spring? What is the best thing about spring?

Sentence knowledge: Help children count the number of words in each sentence.

Word knowledge (phonics): Look at the word *see* on any page. Ask the children to think of words that rhyme with *see*. (bee, sea, he, me, knee, tea)

Word recognition: Ask children to point to the word *see* on page 5. Ask children to find the word *see* on other pages.

Extending ideas

Grow eggshell heads: Give each child an empty eggshell with the top cut off. Curl a piece of pipe cleaner to make a base, and stick it to the bottom of the eggshell. Draw a face on the eggshell. Put some potting compost in the eggshell, and then sprinkle in some grass seeds. Cover the seeds with more soil and water lightly (It may take 10 days for the seeds to germinate.). When the seeds begin to sprout, put the eggshell heads on a sunny window ledge.

In this book

Topic words
bees
blossoms
buds
daffodils
ducklings
kites
lambs
nests
piglets
puddles
rain
rainbows
tadpoles
tulips
umbrellas
wellington boots

Topic
spring

High-frequency words
a
can
see
you

Sentence stem
You can see _____.

Ask children to read these words:
buds   p. 4
daffodils   p. 5
nests   p. 9
ducklings   p. 10
piglets   p. 12